D0912909

Volleyball

BY MATT DOEDEN

AMICUS HIGH INTEREST ❖ AMICUS INK

Amicus High Interest and Amicus Ink are imprints of Amicus
P.O. Box 1329, Mankato, MN 56002
www.amicuspublishing.us

Library of Congress Cataloging-in-Publication Data
Doeden, Matt.
 Volleyball / Matt Doeden.
     pages cm. – (Summer Olympic sports)
 Includes index.
 Summary: "Presents information about volleyball in the
Olympics including rules for playing, and overview of indoor
and beach volleyball, and well-known players such as
Misty May Treanor and Kerri Walsh Jennings"– Provided by
publisher.
ISBN 978-1-60753-811-0 (library binding)
ISBN 978-1-60753-900-1 (ebook)
ISBN 978-1-68152-052-0 (paperback)
1. Volleyball–Juvenile literature. 2. Olympics–Juvenile
literature. I. Title.
 GV1015.34.D64 2016
 796.325–dc23
                                        2014045804

Editor: Wendy Dieker
Series Designer: Kathleen Petelinsek
Book Designer: Aubrey Harper
Photo Researcher: Derek Brown

Photo Credits: Elsa/Getty Images cover; Elsa/Getty Images
5; Hulton Archive/Getty Images 6; Dave Martin/AP/Corbis
9; Chris O'Meara/AP/Corbis 10; Associated Press 13; Chris
O'Meara/AP/Corbis 14; Chris O'Meara/AP/Corbis 16-17;
Cheng Min/xh/Xinhua Press/Corbis 19; Olivier Prevosto/
TempSport/Corbis 20; Associated Press 23; Doug Pensinger/
Getty Images 24-25; Jae C. Hong/AP/Corbis 26; Visionhaus/
Corbis 29

HC 10 9 8 7 6 5 4 3 2
PB 10 9 8 7 6 5 4 3 2 1

Table of Contents

Going for Gold

Thump! The ball sails through the air. Set!
Players on both sides rush toward the net.
Spike! The crowd roars. It's match point!
This is volleyball at the Olympic Games.
Which team will win? Every four years,
players from around the globe gather to go
for the gold medal.

US indoor player Megan Hodge bumps the ball in the 2012 gold-medal match.

People of all ages play
volleyball. These kids play
on an outdoor court.

 How high is an Olympic volleyball net?

A New Game Grows

People have been serving and setting volleyballs for more than 100 years. In 1895, American William G. Morgan made up the game. People wanted a team sport that was easy and fun. Morgan raised up a tennis net. Teams used their hands to **volley** a ball back and forth over the net. The new game was a hit.

 It stands 7.97 feet (2.4 m) for men. Women play with a net standing 7.3 feet (2.2 m).

Volleyball basics are simple. One team serves the ball. The other team tries to knock it back over the net. They can hit it up to three times. Bump! Set! Spike! Players run, dive, and leap. Teams score points when the ball touches the ground on the other team's side. They also score if the other team hits the ball **out of bounds**.

 Do teams have to hit the ball three times?

Martins Plavins of Latvia dives for the ball in the 2012 Olympics.

 No! Sometimes they hit it back after one or two hits. That can be a big surprise!

An indoor volleyball is about
25 inches (63.5 cm) around.

Indoor Volleyball

Soon this new game spread to Europe. The **FIVB** formed in 1947. This group makes rules for volleyball around the world. The FIVB hosted the first world championship games in 1949. Teams from around Europe played to win. The Soviet Union was the winner. Teams were getting ready to make volleyball an Olympic sport.

The 1964 Olympics were in Japan. They featured the first Olympic indoor volleyball games. Both men and women had teams. The Japanese women thrilled their fans. They won all five of their **matches** to earn the gold medal. The Soviet Union ruled the men's teams. They won eight of their nine matches to claim the gold medal.

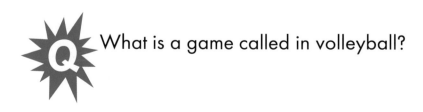 What is a game called in volleyball?

In the 1964 Olympics, the US women battled the home team in Japan. Japan won the match.

 Games are called matches. Matches are made of three or five **sets**. The team that wins the most sets wins the match.

Evgeniya Startseva of Russia serves the ball in the 2012 Olympics.

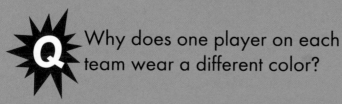

Q Why does one player on each team wear a different color?

The indoor volleyball game is all about power. It is a battle of teams of six. Fans love the big hits and **digs**. Teams try to set up powerful spikes. These smashing hits can zoom at 80 miles per hour (129 km/h)! Members of the other team leap for a block. Who will win the point?

That player is called the **libero**. This is the team's best defender. He or she can substitute into the back row at any time.

The 2012 men's indoor gold-medal match was a classic. Brazil led Russia two sets to zero. In the third set, Brazil led 22 to 19. Three points to gold. But Russia fought back hard. They won the set! Then they won the next two sets! Russia won the gold! It was one of the greatest comebacks in Olympic history!

Russian blockers defend a spike from Brazil in the 2012 gold-medal match.

Beach Volleyball

Sun. Sand. Action. Another kind of volleyball was also growing. Casual games on the beach had turned serious. With only two players on a team, the action in beach volleyball is fast and furious. The basics of the beach game are the same as indoor. But it is very different on the sand. It is a contest of quickness and teamwork.

Canada's Annie Martin dives for the ball in the 2012 Olympics.

The beach volleyball stadium
was on Bondi Beach in Sydney,
Australia, for the 2000 Olympics.

 What is a **demo sport**?

Beach volleyball was a demo sport in the 1992 Olympics. Fans loved the fast-paced action. Each match was a two-on-two beach battle. There was a lot more open space. Players flew around the court. They dove. They spun. They jumped. In beach volleyball, players can't focus on just one area of the game. They must be able to do it all very well.

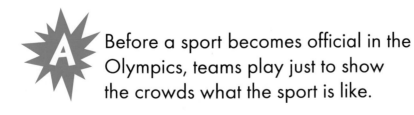

Before a sport becomes official in the Olympics, teams play just to show the crowds what the sport is like.

Beach volleyball became an Olympic sport in 1996. Twenty-four men's teams and 18 women's teams hit the sand. Two US teams faced off in the men's final round. Charles "Karch" Kiraly and Kent Steffes won the match for the gold. Brazilians Sandra Pires and Jackie Silva took the women's title. They faced another team from Brazil.

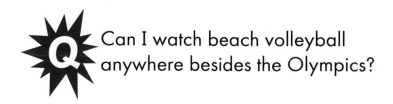
Can I watch beach volleyball anywhere besides the Olympics?

US player Kent Steffes hits the ball past a block in the 1996 Olympic gold-medal match.

 Yes! The top players compete on the pro tours in both North America and Europe.

The beach is where volleyball's stars are made. The sport's first superstar was Karch Kiraly. Kiraly helped the indoor team win gold medals for the United States in 1984 and 1988. Then he switched to the beach. He helped get the sport noticed. FIVB named him the greatest volleyball player of the 20th century!

Gold medalist Karch Kiraly is a leader in US volleyball.

Gold medalist Kerri Walsh Jennings helps her team win gold in the 2012 Olympics.

The US team of Misty May-Treanor and Kerri Walsh Jennings may be one of the greatest teams ever. These two women earned gold in 2004 and 2008. They didn't lose a single set either year! They finally lost a set in 2012. But they still won all their matches. They took their third gold medal that year.

Olympic Glory

On the court or at the beach, volleyball is a thrilling sport. The Olympics are a great way to see the world's best athletes show their skills. So kick back and watch your nation's teams. Cheer as they try to bump, set, and spike their way to Olympic glory.

US volleyball stars Misty May-Treanor (left) and Kerri Walsh Jennings (right) show off their gold medals in 2012.

Glossary

demo sport A sport that is played for show; players do not win medals if they win.

dig A play in which a player saves a hard shot from hitting the ground.

FIVB In French, it is short for Fédération Internationale de Volleyball, which is the International Federation of Volleyball. This group makes the rules for international volleyball games.

libero A defensive specialist in indoor volleyball who wears a different colored shirt and follows some different rules from the other players.

match A volleyball game made up of sets; most matches are three or five sets.

out of bounds The space outside the official court.

set A part of a volleyball match; most sets go up to 15, 21, or 25 points.

volley To hit a ball back and forth.

Read More

Butterfield, Moira. *The Olympics: Events.*
Mankato, Minn.: Sea-to-Sea Publications, 2012.

McIntyre, Abigael. *An Insider's Guide to
Volleyball.* New York: Rosen Central, 2015.

Peters, Stephanie True. *Great Moments in the
Summer Olympics.* New York: Little, Brown and
Co., 2012.

Websites

Beach Volleyball | Olympic.org
www.olympic.org/beach-volleyball

The Game | International Volleyball Federation
*www.fivb.org/thegame/TheGame_Volleyball
OlympicGames.htm*

Volleyball | Olympic.org
www.olympic.org/volleyball

Every effort has been made to ensure that these websites are appropriate for children. However, because of the nature of the Internet, it is impossible to guarantee that these sites will remain active indefinitely or that their contents will not be altered.

Index

About the Author

Author and editor Matt Doeden has written hundreds of children's and young adult books. Some of his books have been listed among the Best Children's Books of the Year by the Children's Book Committee at Bank Street College. Doeden lives in Minnesota with his wife and two children.